# Very Thought Provoking Poems and Poetry vol. 2

Very Thought Provoking Poems and Poetry vol. 2
© 2007 Kingdom World Enterprises Publishing

ISBN 978-0-6151-5992-8

All Scripture quotations, unless otherwise indicated, are taken from the Holy Bible, King James Version. All Rights Reserved

For General information on our other products and services please Contact our customer care department below.

Kingdom World Enterprises™
Houston, TX 77047
832.704.4218 mob
832.553.2747 fax
tcade@houston.rr.com

# _Acknowledgements_

First I give honor, and glory to the only God that ever died and rose again. I thank him for his unfailing love and his word that many have tried to discredit but could not. I thank him for always keeping his word and for dwelling amongst his people. I'm grateful that a holy and righteous God would want to be intimate and commune with humanity, despite our shortcomings and frailties. I most of all thank him for being real, not a statue, not some picture in a church, and not some man in a confession booth. Despite all the things that I have been through and there has been a lot, without God's help and provision I would have been dead a long time ago.

I also would like to give thanks to the people that I've come across in life who had a huge impact on me.
Thank you to my Pastor Bernard Womack, and First Lady Vanessa Womack. For all your correction, rebuke, and tough love, that was given when it was necessary. I thank you for the example of integrity, character, and honesty. May God Bless you in all that you do. The Church took me in and disciplined me, covered me, and became my birthing place, and I am forever grateful.

To Greg Davis for the fellowship and prayers through the years, and for being a Christ like example to me, To Marvin, Marlon Davis, Ed Henderson, Joe Livingston, Fredrick and Vatchel Young for your financial support, Curtis and Tracia Washington for assisting with the kids when we had no one else, Fred Atwood, Zig Ziglar, Cullen Wilson, and Prophet Aaron Cleburne for speaking powerful words of wisdom over my life, Crossroads Cathedral, Pastor Garrett and Greater Mount Zion, to Hill song

Choir for their anointed cd's, Brooklyn Tabernacle Choir, Pastor
Adrian Rodgers,
To Pastor Torres for your prophetic words, Joyce Meyers for your
encouraging literature, Jack Canfield, and Granddad and family in
Lufkin.

Very special thanks to all the men and women who fought for civil
rights in America, who broke barriers concerning separation and
unity. Thanks to all the organizations that counsel and support
women who have been battered, molested, raped, and abused.

# In Memory of

**Clyde Kinsey Jr.**

**Georgia Rideaux**

**Shamekia Allen**

# Table of Contents

## Scripture
- Blended Together
- Whose Image
- Black Word Association
- Your Prayers
- Get Rich Schemes
- The Blood Saver Her
- The Outlook on Nudity
- Sundays
- The Wrong Funeral Message

## Scripture
- What Type of Church
- Beauty
- Ask him
- The Great I Am
- Catch
- I Wish
- History or His Story
- You Naughty Girl
- Unfulfilled

## Scripture
- The Fear of Heights
- I Should Have Stayed
- Just Like Joseph
- Fear
- Just Be Patient
- Force To Be Reckoned With
- I Wish He Could See Me Now
- Please Don't

*Scripture*
- Because of Man
- I See
- Poverty Mind
- Subconscious Sight
- Teenage Killers
- Will Marriage Cure Lust
- Something is Missing
- I Cant Die Like This
- Are You Guilty of Child Abuse

*Scripture*
- Deceitfulness
- These Overwhelming temptations
- The Lottery versus Tithing
- State Dependant
- No More Excuses
- It Pays to Travel
- The Company You Keep
- The Men of Old
- The War Within In

*Scripture*
- Head Held High
- He Sees It all
- None For Me Thanks
- Stand Alone
- Domestic Violence
- Skin All In
- You Need to be Fired
- Its Shocking
- Pentecostal Peacocks

*Scripture*
- Desire Righteousness
- Heaven or Hell
- Horror Outside America
- My First Sex Teacher
- One Man
- When I Die
- Methods of Death
- Counsel Me
- Don't Shake My Hand

*Scripture*
- The Nag
- Learn The Distinction
- The Power of Two
- Shhhhh!
- Anger Motivates
- You Assume
- Just Forgive
- Hollywood Help Us
- Jonah

*Scripture*
- The Benefits of Marriage
- I'm Opposed
- The Forgotten 50's
- I'll Have My Mansion Now
- Poor Sampson
- The Hell Deception
- Are You Really Free
- A Force to Reckoned With
- Is My Opinion Too Strong
- I Love The Underdogs

### Scripture

- The Remedy For Your Sickness
- Lead Us Not Into Temptation
- Their Definition of Black
- 1 is the loneliest number
- Whose Sin is Greater
- Plantation Behavior
- You Remind me
- Based on a true story
- Spreading

### Scripture

- Dictation
- Don't Get Bitter, Just Get Better
- The Profession
- Strike
- Time Stands Still
- Politically Incorrect
- What Are You Waiting For
- It's the Simple Things
- Boyfriends Versus Husbands

*For whoso findeth me findeth life, and shall obtain favour of the Lord .*

*Proverbs 8:35*

Kingdom

Publishing

# *Foreword*

Sometimes as we journey through life we deal with negative situations and circumstances. Although life can have ups and downs I do believe we can learn from every experience. In the past I would spend time harping over wrongs that were done unto me, until I got into God's word, and essentially got an understanding. God says to bless and curse not, and when someone misuses or slanders you, God says to pray for those people. So instead of having a get you back spirit, I actually put my feelings down on paper.

Understand this, all opposition is not bad. When you are opposed long enough, you will get livid enough to change the situation. When people are denied employment, some will start their own company. When someone gets tired of riding in the back of the bus, they will refuse to give up their seat, and then the door for change is opened.

Now I understand that not all things that have happened in my life are the result of someone else's doing. Some things were from Satan and some were self inflicted, regardless the word of God says that **ALL THINGS WORK TOGETHER FOR GOOD TO THEM THAT LOVE THE LORD AND ARE CALLED ACCORDING TO HIS PURPOSE. (Romans 8:28)** We are to give God praise in all situations, because just when you think life didn't turn out right, God is always working behind the scenes. God is always perfecting your character, integrity, faithfulness and commitment. He loves you so much that he allows some things to happen in your life so you can grow and mature and draw closer to him.

If anyone ever tells you the moment you give your life to Christ all your troubles disappear, they are preaching a false doctrine. The Bible never indicates our walk would be easy, but it does indicate without faith we cannot please God. Always know that you are not the only person going through difficulties and transitions, because the body of Christ is a family, and when one hurts we all hurt.

We can overcome because Christ empowers you here on earth to live victoriously and to be a witness. Understand this, with success comes trials, with power comes responsibility, with fame comes attention, and with the anointing comes accountability. If you want anything from God, trust me it will cost you! When you are his representative here on earth His name is also on the line, so God must change you into the image of His son, Jesus Christ.

*And God said, "Let us make man in our image, after our likeness; and let then have dominion…*

*Genesis 1:26*

Vol. $2$

# *Freedom of Speech*

Our Freedom of Speech
Should not be a license to abuse
To spew out our ignorance on the evening news
Talk show host claim this is a free nation
To use speech that involves humiliation
To attack another race
Based on how they behave
Is to take away freedom, and to enslave
Saying whatever, whenever
Regardless of how it sounds
Thinking its wisdom, while sounding like clowns

Freedom to curse, saying four letter words
Saying this is America, well it's still absurd
The word freedom should mean you're free
Free from ignorance and futility
In America you do have the right to speak your mind
But not to the point of acting deaf, dumb, and blind

## *Hyper Sensitive*

Should a talk show host be fired?
If he was considered a racist
And if he claims the comments he made
Were on a joking basis
If he spoke something that was touted as bigotry
Could he have picked this up
From the televised rap imagery
Have we become so sensitive?
That when negative comments are made
We immediately think lawsuit
And how we can get paid
If you must fire someone
You must hold everyone responsible
Instead of sending out activist
Attorneys and constables

If I use the N word constantly
Around my very own kind
When another race uses it surely I won't mind
Why get offended at something we allow
And when things erupt negatively we wonder how
When I was growing up, I was taught to have think skin
To not take this world seriously, because they will
offend
So let people say what they will say
Instead of cursing them out, bless them and pray

# The Ultimatum

Ladies always remember this!
No ring, no sex
No ring, no respect
No ring, no caressing
No ring, no undressing
No ring, no enjoyment
No ring, your deployment

And to the men!
If she exposes, postpone the wedding
Until the atmosphere is a Godly setting
If she dresses provocatively
She might be sleazy
And getting her in bed will be too easy
Several children by several men
You might want to rethink this again

There will always be signs, just pay attention

# *The Definition of Crazy*

I use to think that everyone who was considered crazy
Would speak to themselves and lose all self-control
But I was wrong!

The crazies are not those in hospitals or asylums
But any person having sex without a condom
Nowadays sex is like Russian roulette
Or like a box of chocolates
You never know what you may get

What's even worse is, someone will say I love you
Knowing they are infected
And claim Sweetheart don't you trust me
To screw me unprotected

There is not enough love in the world to ignore
common sense
Even if the kissing is passionate, and the love making
intense

# *Corrupt Authority*

Who gave you the authority?
Even the superiority
To overrule a helpless minority
How can you lead
When you're not able to follow
Such simple commands so easy to swallow
We are not recipients of empty promises and words
Hastily spoken nouns and verbs
Who gave you this position
You who no longer have any vision

You were created in splendor
But was sidetracked with pride
God found hidden agendas inside
As you portrayed a Jekyll and Hyde
You dictate who can vote
Who can elect, who is worthy of respect
Dictating who shall praise you and raise you up high
Your authority is corrupt like a Babylonian empire
And this is the reason you were sentenced to hell fire

# *The Gifts*

God placed the gifts in you
So you could glorify his name
But if you wander confused without vision
God is not the blame
Some are gifted to create wealth
Some are gifted to heal
There is never a reason to be jealous of another
Because God gave all of us skill
Every person has hidden talents within
Ask God to reveal them
And your journey will begin

Regardless of race, age, or gender
We all were created in Gods splendor
But there is a difference for those tuned in
Because the bible says a mans gifts
Will bring him before men
Or should I say kings, princes, even high places
Only holding bills with high numbers
And large faces

# The Laws

Man made laws were passed
To keep men under control
But the ones who make them
Constantly break them
The Ten Commandments
Are laws without any flaws
But are they relevant for our generation

The Answer is yes!

God says thou shall not kill
Yet a man tells a woman to abort
Doctors are making millions in clinics
Like some kind of sport
God says to not murder
So we put the weapons away
But are still guilty
By the malicious words we say

# *You Need to Listen*

If two people are talking at the same time
Vital information can't be heard
And if you claim you know it all
You are unwise and being absurd
You cannot possibly know everything
So please listen as you hear
God gave you two ears
So every message could be clear

Good communication is vital to your success
There's no misunderstandings, no errors to confess
If you listen very well, you will communicate better
Every word, phrase, paragraph and letter

# *History Repeating Itself*

There was bloodshed, humiliation
Shackles and chains
Separation among family members
And dismembered remains

We cried out for freedom
And when it was granted
We have ceased to grow and expand
Because of what was planted

Instead of progressing forward
We seem to retract
Our own people claiming to be pimps
Self-esteem and dignity no longer intact

Some gave their lives
So you could vote and go to college
And not still be a slave
Foolish and rejecting knowledge

*Fear God and keep his commandments, for this is the whole duty of man.*

*Ecclesiastes 12:13*

# *Don't Turn Away*

Don't turn your eyes away
When you see a crime in progress
Why pretend you didn't see it
Only to carry a burden upon your chest
Call the police and don't worry about retaliation
God is your refuge and also your salvation
The enemy of this world would love
For you to just to ignore
All rapes and robberies, and just let evil soar

We use to be a nation
That wouldn't hesitate to get involved
We spoke out against evil
And saw those problems be resolved
But fear has gripped and paralyzed this nation
We are afraid of the bad guys and their affiliations
When we see a victim being victimized
We pretend we don't see and then act surprised

# _Celebrities Are Not God_

God says in his word rather clearly
That as God he is jealous
Giving praise to athletes and secular movie stars
And for him were not even zealous

The tabloids chart their every move
Following them to clubs
Monitoring their every groove
Staking outside their residents like Sherlock Homes
As paparazzi with cameras begin to roam

The country can be at war
But breaking news will cover a divorce
Married for the fifth time
And the sleazy tabloids were the source

Celebrities departing to jail
Will get more coverage than an election
We have simply lost our love for God
And upon them we place our affection

# *Affairs of the Heart*

How foolish was I to mistake the truth for a lie
Every word said that I was fed
Caused me to be mislead
I gave my entire heart from the very start
Only to have it torn apart

I provided, even subsided
Until your new man and I collided
The late night calls, and the laughter
As if my feeling didn't matter
No affection, just rejection
Until there was conception
Another child outside marriage
By two different men, equals more sin

Now you will be labeled a single mother
Just like all the others
Who ran to the arms of another lover!
Daytime talk shows said it best
Pertaining to DNA test
An affair on the side
In its first stage causes pride
Afterwards it causes shame
Because there is no one left to blame

Several minutes of pleasure
Caused a happy home to be destroyed
Trust that was no longer void

So who will remain among the guilty?
Who will be named among the filthy?
Ask yourself was it worth it to be a statistic
Let's be realistic
A child needs both parents
To become more stable and able
But sometimes our decisions
Have heartbreaking repercussions
Because we fail to follow instructions

## _Dead or Alive_

Has anyone ever told you?
That risk takers are consistent moneymakers
Very persistent and overachieving record breakers
Willing to take losses
To be exempt from arrogant bosses
They constantly take chances
In order to make financial advances
Whether it be mutual funds or stocks
They think outside the box
From 401k's to traditional IRA's
Their dividends are compounding for days
A risk taker may encounter
Several highs and lows and numerous foes
In the meantime, the interest still grows
Cash still flows, abundant harvest in perfect rows
If you don't takes risk, this means you are secure
Will your job be here tomorrow, Are you sure?

Job security is uncertain
They unexpectedly will close the curtain
You need to break out of your mold
And pray for a spirit that's bold
Do something with your life before you become old
See yourself moving out
Of your crack-infested neighborhood
And stop making the same tired excuse
I would if I could
Well you can if you rise and open your eyes

And come away from the dead
That's surrounded with flies
The very company you keep
Will determine the wealth you reap
The alive are very active
While the dead remain sleep
But there are decisions to be made
If you must get paid
You have decide, if you will swallow your pride
Step out on faith or be like a coward and hide
Every fear you have face it, then replace it
With dreams and visions and more concise decisions

No more pink slips, attached with paper clips
That sends you on head-trips, so get a grip
If you speak about prosperity to those with no clarity
Some may understand, but this is a rarity

Talk to those, with similar goals
And similar souls taking on similar roles
 I know you are sick and tired
With the threat of being fired
When you are nowhere near the age of being retired
God has given us the power to get wealth
So reexamine your self

# Girlfriends Verses Wives

What causes you to prosper faster?
A wife or a girlfriend
Girlfriends are good companions
Wives are the perfect blend

A girlfriend is more like a roommate
A wife is an investment
Girlfriends are good for dates
Wives are the best assessments

When you argue with a girlfriend
The door is open for you to leave
It's totally different with a wife
God commanded you to cleave

A girlfriend is more like a Chevy
A wife is more like a Benz
A girlfriend has a return policy
A wife's warranty never ends

With a girlfriend you spend money together
With a wife, assets are combined
With a girlfriend you grow together
With a wife you intertwine

## *Until*

I use to think that love
Was found in the arms of a stranger
Until I fell in love with
The one born in a manger
You are void of peace
Until you meet the prince
He surpasses all understanding
And all common sense

I thought celebrities were famous
Until I met the **KING**
Not the one from Graceland
But from heaven, who took me under his wing
Trust me, sex is completely overrated
Until you meet the one who created it
And knowing means all the difference!

Just as passengers sought to go down with the Titanic
Since he is fearless, we have no reason to panic
But unlike that famous ship that was taken down by ice
He will not let you go under; he's already paid the price
Until you meet him, you only think you are alive
It is a mirage that vanishes when you open your eyes
What a surprise? I'm telling you that Jesus is real
And you won't experience the full benefits until

## _Unstable_

Some people change addresses
Phone numbers and careers
Marriage partners and beliefs
All in a matter of years

People are looking for you
They don't remember your name
They try to call your residence
But your numbers not the same

One day you're a plumber, the next a mechanic
Women turn you off, the next day you're romantic
You change churches, memberships
And even decisions
Schools, majors, and even religions

## _On Earth as it is in Heaven_

In Heaven there is no sickness, no disease
No lack, bumming or begging please
No anger, discord, or confusion
And a peace of mind is no longer an illusion

Heaven is abounding with the greatest materials
So why on earth are we needy individuals
If there is joy in Heaven, there should be joy on Earth
If there are riches in Heaven, we should posses a
greater net worth
If there is freedom in heaven
On earth we should expect liberation

Heaven is holy, a place of consecration
So even as we live on Earth
We should experience sanctification

Heaven is clean, pure, the glory, the allure
Empowered on the Earth so we can endure

# *No Religion For Me*

No religion for me, since religion is man made
I prefer full sun, instead of partial shade
I need full bloom, and annual development
Not man made truths, which are irrelevant

Instead of being religious and following rules
Follow the carpenter and his unyielding tools
His method has been proven for over 2000 years
Unlike religion which has man concocted fears

Certain men wouldn't accept the truth Jesus spoke
They listened for a second and even took notes
Then decided they would write their own edition
Twisting Biblical accounts with suspicion

*Ask, and it will be given to you; seek and you will find; knock, and it will be opened to you...*

*Matthew 7:7*

## Blended Together

Why do we love sex in the dark, in the park?
In various places, with unfamiliar faces
A new stroke, a new moan
Fingers going in forbidden zones

Do you know God is watching?

Is that man your husband?
Is that woman your wife?
Doing dirty deeds in the motel
What a perverted sight
You are letting a stranger enter in
Only to inject demonic seed
No wonder they just want you for sex
Because demons are filled with greed

And when you say the magic words
When will you marry me?
Or do you even care
They look happy and content
As long as your legs are in the air

Look that person in the eye
Who has no intention of settling down
And tell them you now belong to Christ
And you are sick of being bound

# *Who's Image*

It's a sad sight to see
A grown man beg for spare change
Settling for washing your windows
Its nerve wrecking and strange
Or sometimes they say mister
Can I please pump your gas
A vagabond, drifter and forgotten outcast

How long will you sleep
And wander in the wilderness like sheep
You are in this negative situation
Because you have no connection or relation

Not with family, because with them we cleave
Become super-dependant and never want to leave
Your image is that of Christ, and not of man
He gave you the ability to posses even the land

So don't settle for merely nickels and dimes
Stop washing windows and quit wasting your time
In the image of God, there is nothing but creativity
You can do whatever you want because you have the
ability

## Black Word Association

Why does black rhyme with crack, lack, and attack
Why is it associated with the words smack, and car jack

Obviously the word black
Hs several meanings and unusual signs
Therefore black would also be a synonym
For the corrupt criminal mind
If you are suspected of disloyalty
You are considered blacklisted
When a brother is crossing the street at a red light
The driver is clinching their purse and tight fisted

The illegal selling or buying of merchandise
Is frequently called a black market
And those always accused
Are for obvious reasons the black targets

If you have a black out you lack illumination
And when the darkness falls and nighttime comes
You have extreme aggravation
Black clothing is always worn for mourning
It's associated with death and dying
Even the grim reaper sports black gear
Were struggling, surviving, and still trying

## *Your Prayers*

I'm always mesmerized
When I hear someone say
I've been praying for months
But still experiencing delay
Then they openly reveal
They've prayed to Saint Peter and Saint Jude
Next I attempt to share knowledge
Without being arrogant or rude

The Bible says there is
One mediator between God and man
His name is Jesus, The Christ
His presence is majestic and grand
Dead saints are just that, dead
And if you think they will answer you
You are being mislead

You can confess in a booth for mercy and grace
But the one you're confessing to must lie on his face
He does not have the power to forgive
Despite his priestly attire, Christ is the reason we live
All our prayers and supplications
Must go to the King of Kings
Who is the God of our salvation

## _Get Rich Schemes_

Sometimes I stop at the convenient store
Just for an ice cold drink
And to my surprise there is a very long line
So I pause for a minute and think

Young folk and the elderly are hoping to become rich
Spending $100 to win $5, because they feel the itch
What ever happened to hard work and genuine sweat
You've been playing for years and haven't won yet
What does that tell you; follow hard after your dreams
Because man will lay a snare before you
Like false pyramid schemes
But wealth not earned through hard work
And determination
Will fly away like eagles to a higher elevation

Do you ever watch the shows, as they chronicle the
lives?
Of all the past winners now cries and sighs
They squandered money away as did the prodigal son
Buying expensive cars and jewelry and simply having
fun

# The Blood Saved Her

No element is as vital as the blood
It is our life source, it sustains
When it is shed, it still remains

There was a man who murdered his wife
Because of jealousy he stabbed her with a knife
He placed her body in concrete under a shack
And left her to decay, and never came back

In the process of burying her
The previous stab wound he caused
The blood was spilled, it caused him to pause

He poured bleach on the spot, to eradicate the stain
The more he scrubbed, the more it remained
So he grabbed some paint and began to pour
Mixing different colors on the concrete floor

But just like Cain who tried to erase
After killing Abel and hiding his face
Cain was arrogant, confident and cunning, and brave
But God told him the blood
Was crying out from the grave

# _The Outlook on Nudity_

The body is a work of art as stated by many
Curvaceous and toned, an object to envy
But what about nudity
On reservations and even resorts
Claiming its natural to interact and play sports
This was ok in the beginning of creation
But we live in a society
Where perversion is as high as inflation

There is no way a mother and son
Should see each other nude
Or father and daughter
It's unthinkable and lewd
Still there are those who think it's natural
Even though pedophiles and child predators
Lurk everywhere and that's factual
But the greatest debate is
They allow it in England and also Brazil
But these countries are not our standards
For righteousness, so get real

The word of God is our standard not man's opinion

# _Sunday_

It's Sunday, and many seek out mega churches
To hide in the pews
Possibly to hear the watered down version
Of the gospels good news
A feel good message that never addresses sin
So many go back out, the same way they came in
This was precisely my situation
I wish someone had preached
On shacking up and fornication
I didn't need a message so I could feet great
I needed deliverance and a great escape

We should not forsake the assembly
Of ourselves with other believers
But we should forsake the assembly
Of doubters and underachievers

# The Wrong Funeral Message

Some preachers are people pleasers
And not God pleasers
The pick the wrong sermon at funerals
Like a pair of tweezers
If you know Johnny was a drunk
And undercover pedophile
Don't tell the congregation
You'll see him again in a little while
The bible does not teach
That all men will go to a heavenly place
Narrow is the road
And many refuse walk it straight
I've heard at funerals the preachers say
He is gone to be with the Lord
By the way he was not saved, lived like a heathen
And his life was hard
I guess because someone had it hard in this life
Automatically gains them the right to live with Christ
This a false doctrine written be demons
They are having intercourse with the ignorant
And injecting their semen

Tell the truth about Johnny,
He rejected salvation every time it was presented
He thought the gospel was a joke and never repented

*The Fear of the Lord is the beginning of wisdom*

*Proverbs 9:10*

# What Type of Church

Jesus said man's tradition stops his power
And this is so rampant in this final hour
Do you attend a church?
That believes God no longer heals
Rather than receiving healing
You put faith in your pills
The doctor gives you advice
But Jesus is the great physician
He says by his stripes you are healed
So you can now boast in this position
Do you attend a church?
That preaches God is not into prosperity
So everyone remains broke, blind with no clarity
They believe in giving, but expect nothing in return
When you give you receive
Sometimes more than what you earn
Do you attend a church?
That preaches prophets no longer exist
This is divine revelation from God
That surely you don't want to miss
Go to a church that's alive and not dead
Where there is plenty vision
And the sheep's get fed

# *Beauty*

She has a gorgeous face, pretty brown eyes
And nice full lips
A well-toned body, a radiant smile
And wide voluptuous hips
No wrinkles, no blemishes
Just an array of sex appeal
The glamour of a forties Hollywood diva
That just doesn't seem real

On the outside her beauty is stunning
For many men to see
But does all these physical attributes describe beauty
The heart surpasses the face
Just as the inner surpasses outer
But the most beautiful parts
Can still make one a doubter
In your early years
Your looks will open doors and never fade
But as you age gracefully
More makeup will be added to hide every shade
The very looks women treasure
Is not really a treasure at all
Because time does not procrastinate
Discriminate, nor stall
The day will come
When your so-called beauty shall rapidly pass

When you are laid in a casket
The guest will walk by and ask
What happened to her?
She doesn't look that beautiful now.

# *Ask Him*

Who am I, and why was I created
Two familiar questions that are greatly debated
You are a person that was created to love
The almighty God who reigns from above
Without a secure relationship with Christ
There will be unanswered questions about this life
Like why are people without food and protection?
Worldwide chaos with political subjection
You may wonder why divorces seem to be on the rise
A man marries a woman
But is a homosexual in disguise
Who do some criminals commit crimes?
And then are set free, the guilty go unpunished
The victims receive the third degree
Every question, thought, or comment God has a reply
He knows why you were born, and when you must die
Don't just wonder about life, get to know him
personally
So he can give you knowledge and fill you spiritually
Just ask him, because he is never to busy for your needs
If you lack wisdom or peace
Even if you hunger, he feeds
He loves you and just longs for your intimate
conversations
To spend eternity with him, and to never experience separation

## *The Great I Am*

The most intimate moments I ever had
Were with a man
Who walks, talks, teaches and understands
He does not argue
Leave me neither empty nor isolated
I laugh with him, cry with him
And marvel at the things he created
He is my friend, my husband, and by bodyguard
The prince of peace, and the Lord of Lords
No one can come between us, we are forever connected
I abide under the shadow of the Almighty
So I'm always protected
He loved me when I was drinking and sleeping around
I was stealing, cursing, abusive and bound
Still he overlooked my faults, and showed me his grace
Although I was found guilty, he died in my place
I would marry him 1000 times, and never consider
divorce
Separated from this world I would have no remorse
He conquered everything we suffer; it was nailed at the
cross
So we would be victorious and never at a loss
Death should not be feared, instead celebrated
Because on earth for him you patiently waited


You go to work stressed yet claim you are blessed
Are you aware God wants you to have the best?

Why should you suffer with the curse of hypertension?
When the covenant with Abraham was Gods invention

Your health should be robust and your joy overflowing
Because of a God who is all seeing and all knowing
He knows we should live happy and healthy
And at some point in this life wise and wealthy
We are supposed to be imitators of Christ
The Son of God who gives abundant life

# _Catch_

Have you ever heard the phrase?
The early bird catches the worm
You must be swift to move
Like a deadly virus or germ

If you ever get replaced or fired
Tell your boss thanks
Now doors will really open for you
As you move up in the ranks

A turtle will take his time
But you must be like the hare
A turtle does not pay attention
While the hare is keenly aware

The world is full of treasures
And opportunities just ready to hatch
Many of them can be yours
If you are able to catch

# *I Wish*

I wish we could all get along, sing a new song
And stop treating each other wrong
I wish love could last forever with no divorce
Soft-spoken words with no remorse
I wish the crime rates would drastically decrease
All abortions and teen pregnancies cease
I wish more people would submit to authority
Even the majority, this should be a priority
I wish fervent prayer were back in schools
To have order and go by the rules
I wish our precious lives were valued more
So criminals could not soar, the lions could not roar
I wish more people were born again
And their lives not contaminated with sin
And say the end
I wish Eve had resisted the garden temptation
Instead Hell had a glorious celebration
I wish all those who hunger, in this world were fed
And out of all the words we spoke
The truth would be said
I wish those that were saved could be brave
And take the gospel to roads unpaved
I wish all the rich would give a portion to the poor
Walk a day in their shoes and not ignore
I wish there was no such thing as self-pity or pride
And asking would be easier to decide
I wish we could all worship the same Messiah
Who heals and delivers and can take us higher

I wish there was neither colors black nor white
So racism could be put to a flight
I wish no single race ever felt superior
And if so they could also feel inferior

# *History or His Story*

Even in this great country
You need to be cautious about information
That is broadcast to individuals
Across liberal T.V. stations

Some news will be reported
Saying we are at battle
While deception happens on our own soil
The serpent slitters and his tail rattles

Even our greatest leaders have hidden agendas
Convincing Americans otherwise
To remain calm and surrender

Do you know that many textbooks!
Were actually written by crooks
I say crook because of deception
Misleading and psychological interjection

We use to pledge allegiance to the flag
But now freedom of speech, is an order to gag

# *You Naughty Girl*

She's wears the lowest cut blouses
The tightest jeans
She wants to infiltrate your thoughts
And your dreams
She is a Naughty, Naughty girl

You see her at work
Her dirty talking
You take a second look
When you see her walking
She is a Naughty, Naughty girl

You see her at church
She's on the back pew
Instead of reading the bible
She watching you
She is a Naughty, Naughty girl

Her thoughts are rather wicked
An evil mind
You better pass her up
She's not your kind
She is a Naughty, Naughty girl

# _Unfulfilled_

Never in my life
Have I had a job that was fulfilling!
The hours were always long
And the pay was never appealing
The people were always complacent
Some pessimistic and content
If the job didn't pose a challenge
Then my attention was bent
If I am not the boss, I fill miserable
And slip into bouts of depression
So I have to pretend in front of coworkers
With a smile and fake expression
I do little as possible, until my day is finished
I'm torn apart inside
My hopes and dreams diminish
I know God created us all different
So my talent can't be wasted
My visions and dreams are very explosive
And some success I've tasted
I know there are millions out there
Who feel exactly like me!
That success is not necessarily a well paying job
Or college degree
But is about following your destiny!

*Thou shalt love thy neighbor as thyself. Love worketh no ill to his neighbor.*

*Romans 13:9,10*

## The Fear of Heights

The world is large and very impressive
With vast opportunities
So you must be aggressive
Anyone with drive or the passion to succeed
Must we willing to go the distance by any creed
If you know your family
Is barely making ends meet
You need to overcome your fears
Without being discreet
No one should suffer
In the greatest country on earth
God placed tremendous gifts
Inside you even from birth
You only think you're disadvantaged
Because you may lack education
Maybe you're a minority or democratic
But there's is still elevation

# I Should Have Stayed

Ladies have you ever had a man
And during your relationship
He had no ambition
You looked at all his dead end jobs
For he was in a hopeless condition
He had no desire to further his education
At least this is what you believed
He always spoke about the dreams he had
Those, which were never conceived
So you decided to break up
Because your friends said he was not you type
They said girlfriend you can do much better
And you chose to believe the hype

But now some years have passed
And this brother has exited your mind
But sometimes you still wonder
If things would have improved with time
But then you run into an old friend
At the corner newspapers stand
And she tells you your ex
Is now a successful businessman
She heard he was worth millions
And his company is even worldwide
For a minute you're speechless
And then utterly left surprised

Now you realize you should have stayed
He wasn't that bad, if only you would have prayed
Because the man you have now
Is happy to just have sex
It's been years; and what do you have
No marriage, no commitment and no respect

## *Just Like Joseph*

Although you were raised in the ghetto
You know your destiny is before you
Many people have counted you out
But the world won't be able to ignore you
Your vision is precise and profound
But don't tell everyone about it
To some it will make sense, for others it will astound
And still some won't cease to doubt it

Just like Joseph, he shared with his brothers
They immediately begin to resent him
While the devil was accusing him of explicit sex
The Lord himself was reinventing him
If you are like Joseph your name will be great
Through the trials victory stands at the gate

# _Fear_

What is Fear?
False Evidence appearing real
No amount is beneficial
Regardless to how you feel

What are our Fears?
There is fear of failure, and fear of success
Fear of life, and fear of death
Fear of being married, and fear of being alone
Fear of being childless, someone to call your own
Fear of being loved, and fear of being rejected
Fear of speaking the truth, and fear of being corrected

Fear of launching out, fear of achieving
Fear of understanding God, fear of believing

## *Just Be Patient*

How long are you willing you wait
To find that perfect mate
Are you willing to lower your standards?
To become hooked like bait

There is a secret I have discovered
Love God first before seeking a lover
If you love him first
It will be easier to love another

If you ever find a person
Who loves God with all their heart
This will be the one to marry
They will always be by your side
And never want to be apart

## _Force to Be Reckoned With_

I watched as she approached our land
Bringing gust of wind
More than we could stand
All night long the newscasters gave us notice
Telling us how awesome she would be
And where she would focus

They even set a time frame
When she would appear
And when she finally did
It struck disbelief and fear

She pulverized the coast
As the rains poured heavy
And sometime during the middle of the night
She even destroyed the levy

Thousands without power
Missing sons and daughters
Rescue teams search for victims
As corpses floated in the water

## I Wish He Could See Me Now

When my dad died I was still living in my sins
Same old bad habits, same old friends
I was shacking up with my girlfriend
In my comfort zone
Far away from Christ, off on my own
I was at a dead end job
And life was going nowhere
I was at a low point and I started not to care
Then my son was born
And my joy was overflowing
I was very happy and excited knowing
Life was about to change

But I remember growing up
My dad said, "**You will always be a thug**"
Hanging out smoking cigarettes or selling drugs
I think sons always seek for their father's approval
And when we don't receive it
Its back to sinning as usual
By this time my son was getting older
And I was getting bolder
Still I had a lot of weight on my shoulder
I was not making the amount of money I desired
And to top it all off I was fired
I wonder what dad thought of me then

The news came to me that he finally passed away
I was very upset because I had more to say
I was angry because I was not yet a success
I was trying hard, but my life was still a mess
And one day I had an encounter with another man
He accepted my shortcomings and gave me a plan
He instilled vision and I can't forget purpose
Fear was destroyed and I was no longer nervous
Because my new dad accepted me
By the way his name is Jesus!

## *Please Don't*

Everyday she would come home from school
Just hoping to relax
Always the first one to make it home
Anxious and eager to unpack
She would watch cartoons
Before starting on her assignment
Dreading the late evening
When her home would become a confinement
She would get nervous
Because daddy would make it home
He would give her this animalistic look
Before his fingers would roam
His own daughter he would touch
Committing acts behind close doors
Until she considered herself unclean
And her body was riddled with sores

Some men can't find suitable mates
So their own daughter will become their date
The child screams daddy please don't
He gets on top of her and says in a loud voice I won't
He took her virginity, and no one suspected
He would mess with whores, and sex her unprotected
How could someone whom you respect and trust?
Darken your heart with anger and disgust

This unfortunately would occur on a daily basis
Years would pass
And she would remember those faces
She harbored this secret until graduation
And her perverted dad still had an infatuation

*The Fear of The Lord prolongeth days.*

*Proverbs 10:27*

# *Because of Man*

The floods have become more violent
The talking has become more silent
The suns heat intensifies every summer
Who is the source we don't have to wonder
The winters are now more aggressive
The locations are now more selective
The trees are bearing fruit out of season
And for all this activity there is a reason

The reason is man, who does not understand
What his need for greed has done to our land
The water is unsafe from rivers to seas
And the innocent are exposed to incurable diseases
The air is hazy and filled with pollution
The bigger our SUV's, the bigger the distribution
The world was once a habitat man called paradise
But now people have been reduced to living like mice

# *I See*

With these eyes I see things others may miss
Things visible, invisible, things that disturb
Mirage and hallucinations
I had a dream that manifest in the following days
Every color imaginable with the most beautiful displays
I saw my funeral as they stood in tears
Reminiscing about my life throughout the years
I saw my marriage and did not have a wife
But funny is this thing we call life
I saw the most remote part of this world
And in the midst was the most beautiful girl
I saw something you thought you might have seen
But because my vision is much clearer
I see someone totally different
Than you see when I look in the mirror
This is not the real me, but a reflection
One who speaks well but filled with imperfections
When others see me, they see history
Past, present, and future that is still a mystery
Can you figure out a puzzle?
That has several missing pieces
These words are broken, and the meanings hidden
So the things I see are mysterious and never ceases

# *Poverty Mind*

I was born in it
But refuse to die in it
I was conceived in it
And very familiar with it
I understood it
But would not accept it
At times it depressed me
Discouraged and disgusted me
I tried to escape it
But it followed me

I wanted a better life
While others were content
I was consumed by debt
And not able to pay rent

When my car stopped running
I started walking
When my lights were cut off in the winter
I started talking
Or should I say confessing
The promises of God and his blessing

So-called friends were negative
But I remained positive

I refused to believe
That you can't achieve
Despite the environment in which you live
You can overcome the poverty mindset

## Subconscious Sight

Liquor stores, project whores
Closed doors, negative metaphors
Pay day loans, prepaid phones
Overgrown yards, and boarded up homes
Gold teeth and multiple tattoos
Fake name brand clothing and flea market shoes

Long lines and house slippers
Thugs, felons and syrup sippers
Lottery buyers, but never winning
Different boyfriends and still sinning
Ebonics speech and incorrect grammar
The hardest hit just like a hammer

Do you understand?
What you see will affect your sight
Your subconscious will store and process it
So you will continue in darkness
And never see the light

# Teenage Killers

The same ones you tease on a daily basis
Will be the same ones who remembers your faces
They carefully take notes, and write down names
At night they orchestrate plots
And well thought out games
Surfing the Internet on how to build a bomb
And when the time is right they will ring the alarm

Those same ones who come to school
Always wearing black
It might seem they have forgotten
But most certainly will get you back
Their hearts are filled with resentment
And years of oppressed hate
They likely will kill themselves
As well as a few classmates
Be very observant, notice any usual behavior
And if your life is put on the line, I hope you have a
savior
Those same ones who spend so much time isolated
Are just waiting to explode from the problems created
Mom is too busy, and dad has a lucrative career
These children are crying out for help, can anyone
hear?
Please don't wait until it's too late
Dead bodies on campus from state to state

## _Will Marriage Cure Lust?_

The Bible says it is better
To marry than to burn
Although this is true
There is something you must learn

Some men get married thinking
No more fornication or sexual sinning
Only to find out later
That it was just the beginning

When you were single
You had women by the droves
Now that you are married
You spend more time in your clothes

If you constantly hear
I'm not in the mood
I have a headache
And you can't see me nude

Marriage can actually make lust worst
If there is no intimacy

## _Something is Missing_

If you examine your life closely
Would you say you are successful?
If the answer is yes
Why is it so stressful?

A six figure income, plus health benefits
Very well educated and plenty of common sense
A trophy wife and hefty bank accounts
A company allowance that pays extravagant amounts
Fine tailor suits and expensive meals
Weekend golf while signing million dollar deals
So far life seems to be working out well
But if Christ is missing you are destined for Hell
Most men will proclaim their own goodness
According to Gods word
He utters I've never hurt anyone
Which is vainly absurd
We all fall short of Gods glory
And you are no exception
You were born and shaped in iniquity
Ever since conception
The moral of this story is
You can have all the material success
The entire world has to offer
And certainty FEEL blessed
But without Jesus your existence has no meaning
You may think you are all right
But you are only dreaming

# I Can't Die Like This

I've been to so many funerals
I've begun to lose track
I realize these people are gone
And will never coming back
Some were descent folk; some led a life of crime
But regardless of their lifestyle
They simply ran out of time
As I sit in the pew during the ceremonial service
Something comes to my mind
And makes me nervous
It's not the thought of dying itself
But dying without vision
Without purpose, without destiny
And without precision
It's foolish to dream all your life
And never see them fulfilled
Instead of chasing with persistence
We chase foolishness and get killed

I refuse to go to my grave
Just getting by like the poor
Without walking in the power of God
Which causes me to soar?
So many from the hood died
In this like manner
Below average thinkers
With below average grammar
The lived piddle to post, hand to mouth

And day by day
Applying street wisdom and trickery
Never finding a better way
Although I was born black and surrounded with crack
I consider myself a magnet, born to attract
Wealth, health, longevity and peace
And when all is fulfilled, then my life will cease

# _Are You Guilty of Child Abuse?_

Over 9 million children today are obese
Do you take responsibility
For how you allow them to feast
Can you believe that many kids are diabetics?
Spending less time at the playgrounds
And more with the paramedics

When a child is in his growing stage
Where does he learn about nutrition?
It should be from their parents
Unless they are also in an obese condition

If this is the case, what sense does it make
To say Johnny no snacks before dinner
And please put down that cake
If you have no self control
How can you teach them?
If you don't lead by example
How can you possibly reach them?

You the parent are supposed to be their guide
Instead of saying my child is not fat
You need to swallow your pride

*For every house is builded by some man, but he that built all things is God.*

*Hebrews 3: 4*

# _Deceitfulness_

Everyone is capable of being deceived
I believe
Satan throws out the bait
And we constantly retrieve, like a Labrador
With itching ears we will ignore
Our carnal thoughts that devour like a carnivore

Hitler proved that people can be mislead
Easily brainwashed and unfed
Even in Waco people were deceived
Another man-made God caused them to believe, lies
As we saw the smoke in the skies televised

Small companies do it, even corporations
Look you right in the eye, and lie with no hesitation
Relationships are the worst when someone deceives
you
And when you cry wolf, no one believes you

# _These Overwhelming Temptations_

Spring has gone, and summer is here
Every lost soul awaits the most explicit time of year
From public schools to beaches
Short skirts cling tight like leeches
Strong sexual content at every major event
Displays of perverse behavior without any consent
Televised advertisements based on lust and greed
Therefore America is now growing from a seed
Satan planted it since creation
And until this very day we are robbed as a nation
Society is saturated with filthiness such as pornography
As ordained priest molest little boys with no apology
We accept pedophiles and rapist as ordained civilians
As unreported cases are forgotten by the millions
No wonder America is filled with so much shame and
guilt
We never address issues but cover them like a quilt
So as we turn a deaf ear to problems that plague Gods
people
The righteous remain silent but never overtaken by evil

# The Lottery versus Tithing

You have a better chance to get struck by lightning
I know this may be surprising and frightening
But it is a fact
You spend twenty only to win one
And most people say its just harmless fun

It is really?

The lottery, like other games of chance
Is not like tithing where you can advance
The lottery is purely a game of luck
And after you spend thousands, you still end up stuck
If you were foolish before, money will magnify the fool
The one that's not wise being used as a tool

## State Dependant

Instead of welfare, you should be fairly well
Not lounging by the window
Waiting for the mail
After all the checks is only measly pay
You can double your income starting today

What you need is a plan
That would be fail proof
So you can recapture the years
Of your unfruitful youth

Some are approaching forty
And they are still in the system
But before you sympathize for them
Know that many are not victims

Some choose this way
Because they don't have another
Abusing the system for the needy
Still doing it undercover

# _No More Excuses_

I've met people who hated their job
But yet refused to leave
They are barely making ends meet
And can never meet their needs
They look at natural circumstances
Credit cards, car notes, and rent
And before they can even cash their check
All the money is spent

But for some odd reason
They choose to stay planted
And like a car with no gas
They always seem to be stranded
This is America, the land of opportunity
And there should be an agreement
With passion, drive and unity
If you make far too many excuses
You will awake one day and find yourself useless

## *It Pays to Travel*

If you are like me and you came from the hood
Traveling to distant lands will do you some good
This is partly the reason why I joined the Navy
Because my crack infested hood was about to drive me
crazy

So when my feet first landed in the Middle East
I was served the most scrumptious and amazing feast
It was my very first time seeing a castle
Life was pleasant, peaceful, and no hassle
I also went to the country of France
The mountains, the atmosphere, the romance

I had to renew my mind
Because my thinking was small
I needed the old mind to crumble like the Berlin wall
So I started to take trips, see different views
Trading in my old rags for designer clothes and shoes

# _The Company You Keep_

Whoever walks in knowledge will become wise
If you walk with the simple
You will lack sense and be despised
When you are ready to walk into your new season
You must say goodbye to some old friends
For various reasons
Don't worry! Everyone can't go where you going
Your season is filled with abundance and overflowing
Those who can't see must still walk around blind
But Jesus promised if you seek, and knock
You most certainly would find

Your worse enemies will be those of your own
household
They may just want hay and rubble, but you silver and
gold

## *The Men of Old*

Uncle was creeping
Daddy was cheating
Papa was a rolling stone
Who couldn't stand to be alone

When mama went to work
Daddy snuck out the back door
He had a good wife
But chose to be with a whore

What can I say; he learned it from his pops
Apprehending women just like the cops
They said she likes you, man can't you tell
Blessed with a great marriage, so how did they fail

No respect for papa, papa was a playboy
Spreading his seed, just like a man toy
He died this way, man about the town
In the arms of another still sleeping around

## The War Within

Good thoughts, bad thoughts
Which ones will I exalt?
Raised in the cesspool
It was never my fault

Very depressed, and what not
Full armor on and still felt the guns shots
The battlefield is bloody with no peace
The war in the mind never seems to cease

Pearl Harbor, D Day, and even Vietnam
Is incomparable to this Desert Storm
Prayer, fasting, casting away
All apparent sin that is on display

Plenty of charisma, so I guess I'm a charmer
But on the inside I'm exploding
Like a suicide bomber

*The eyes of The Lord are in every place, beholding the evil and the good.*

*Proverbs 15:3*

# _Head Held High_

It's embarrassing to sleep behind Safeway
Because you have nowhere to stay
You're ashamed to tell someone where you sleep
Behind Wal-Mart, where I sowed is where I reaped
It started raining and my car was my roof
So disappointed and depressed, and aloof

No one was ever aware
That I took a bath at Denny's
And I scraped up some spare change
To get a bite at Wendy's
This is a true story that happened
I just thought I would testify
It was very embarrassing
But my head was held high
I felt I was above standing on the corner begging for
change
So I hit the local pawnshop to rearrange
Not only my thoughts, but also my plan of action
Since circumstances in life can be a distraction
But yet keep your head held high

## _He Sees It All_

Even before you masturbated
Cohabitated, and fornicated
God already knew it was going to happen
He knew you would steal it
Reveal it, and then conceal it;
His eyes don't miss a thing
He watched you as you cheated on the test
Got an A, but never confessed

We always pretend that we are so clever
But I can hear God say no, not ever
Just like Cain committed murder in anger
The grave took life in the form of a stranger
Even when you do taxes, with the wrong additions
He doesn't need to speculate or have suspicions
Because he sees it all, and knows it all
His eyes don't miss

# *None For Me Thanks!*

Who the Son sets free is free indeed
So concerning certain foods
I no longer have a need
No more honey-baked hams
I'll take stir-fry vegetables with no clams
No more chickens with disease
But brown rice and black-eyed peas
Crisp mustard greens, bell peppers, and pinto beans
Less salt, but the garlic I will exalt
Too much butter and I immediately come to a halt
The pig's feet you can have, no more bacon on a slab
Why have bodies out of shape and so full of flab
Half gallons I cream with cake, give me break
For crying out loud my health is at stake
Take a look around, everyone is physically going down
Another late night meal, another pound
No wonder fast food restaurants are filthy rich
A greasy burger is a good sales pitch
Throw in some fries, succulent apple pies
Then add 30 pounds to your hips and thighs
With the excess weight comes excess sickness
The ones who have died before you bear witness
The holidays came and you continued to eat the same
Drunk on food and can't remember their name
When will we learn, those extra calories you have to
burn
You must not depend on food, so I will include
Other dishes to disregard, any meal cooked in lard

Another word for lard is grease
Another word for pig is beast

Due to technology a hot dog may contain an actual dog
Possibly a German shepherd, fox or leopard
It's become so bad man will eat whatever is on his plate
From overcooked eggs to anything out of date
Your God is your belly, decaying flesh that is foul and
smelly
After years of eating garbage, we will look like trash
Or a burning building covered in ash
That same person you wanted as a mate
You now would think twice about even asking them for
a date
We recite for better or for worse
But when you bow down to food you will be under a
curse
Your golden years are now spent in a wheelchair
All because you didn't care
Medication after mediation with no relief
Operation after operation with total grief
In Ecclesiastes it tells us why die before your time
Against the Holy Spirit overeating is a crime
God wants you to be prosperous and well fed
Not confused, full of gluttony and dead

## _Stand Alone_

On the hard issues of life
Sometimes you must stand-alone
But if you stand for what's right
It most certainly will be known
Joining in agreement with popular opinion
Will cause you to lose respect
And not walk in dominion
We are called to walk in righteousness
Regardless to what the world thinks
Its mindset is that of a garbage can and it stinks

If you saw someone steal
Would you turn your head?
And say it's not my business
And go the opposite direction instead
Stand for holiness
Even if everyone around you is sinning
Because if you serve the King of kings
You will always keep on winning

Don't worry about repercussions
The Lord is your banner
Always pray for your enemies
Like Christ in the same manner

## _Domestic Violence_

Regardless to what she says
Don't put your hands on her
Even if she hits you
Simply walk away

Proverbs says a soft word
Will turn away wrath
It might not make any sense
But you do the math

So many men right now
Are incarcerated for life
Because they allowed themselves
To become violent with their wife
Their anger rose up to the point of no control
Because words were said
That was sarcastic and bold

And because men are stronger
They have a tendency to overpower
To become physically abusive
To the point that they devour

But is it really worth it
To spend your life in the Penn
And if you could do it all over
Would you do it again?

# _Skin All In_

It's funny how we categorize people because of race
Instead of showing love and trying to embrace
When you look at old pictures that say WHITES ONLY
Not only at water fountains but rest stops so lonely

Because of skin tone
Should we be filled with hate?
Are we that shallow a people
That we cannot relate

Our skin color is different
But our blood is the same
One nation under God
Should be our aim

Only because of ignorance
Does division between races thrive?
And when our focus is skin color
We simply keep the division alive

# _You Need to be Fired_

Do you make long distance calls on company time?
Take extended lunches on the company's dime
Punch in for hours you don't actually work
You may think it's clever
But whom do you actually hurt

Do you call in sick, when you feel fine?
Gossip uncontrollably and waste precious time
Reports on your desk that you need to conclude
And when you answer the phone, you always seem rude

You expect a raise, but your performance is poor
Would you be disillusioned?
If your boss showed you the door
Your job description requires 100 percent
Every since the day you were hired
So wouldn't it be wise to pull your own weight
Before you end up fired

# *It's Shocking!*

When I think about the time I've wasted
The sin I've tasted
It's shocking!
I've tasted more sin than I've tasted deserts
Very heartbreaking and it hurts
And even when you turn your life over
A new way of doing, a new purpose for pursuing
And you seek righteousness instead of seeking out sin
Evil ways in the company of men
Like a stray dog sin finds its way home
Knocks at the door and hopes you're alone

If the home is not well cleaned, and properly steamed
The assault will begin like a Stephen King dream
God told Cain that sin was crouching at his door
Ready to pounce like a tiger if he wouldn't ignore
Its whispers, its callings, saying come do this
Until it manipulates like Judas, even with a kiss
If you stay in sin too long you'll become like Saul
Not sensitive to Gods voice, and pride caused him to
fall
By any means necessary I had to no longer be bound
I once was lost but now I'm found

# _Pentecostal Peacocks_

They name it and claim it
Blab it and grab it
They say speak what you want
And you can have it

They say decree and you will see
But forget about righteous living
To receive the same blessings
That God is giving

Righteousness is a qualification
Holiness is your meditation
But bless me Lord, Bless me Lord
Is our chanting sensation

In addition to being blessed
Preachers need to preach the cross
So many want end up with tons of money
And at the same time being lost

*"Awake, thou that sleepest, and arise from the dead, and Christ shall give thee light."*

*Ephesians 5:14*

## _Desire Righteousness_

When we came into this world
We were not taught how to be righteous and holy
But instead taught sometimes you have to lie

God said all liars would have
Their part in the lake of fire
Do not follow the crowd;
Let righteousness be your desire
You don't have to sleep with him
To get the annual promotion
Just walk in integrity
And you will avoid the commotion
Let God keep you holy and pure
He will sustain you, for I am sure

Wear your modest apparel and do not expose
When you put on holiness it glows and shows
Be still before the Lord and wait patiently
Desire forever to love him insatiably

## _Heaven or Hell_

Both places are dreadfully real
And both have an expectation
One desires you because of righteous
The other because of sins such as fornication

Man will frequently try to convince you
That Hell exist only in your mind
And teach it's not a literal place
Somewhere you can actually find
Some people have said
There is no such thing as morality
So why would God create a place
That was without immortality

The bible teaches there is a place
So I believe this story
It would take an enormous amount of faith
To believe in some false purgatory

If you are not a believer in God
I understand why you would reject the belief
Just make sure you are completely right
So you don't suffer eternally with grief

## _Horror Outside America_

America is the greatest country
But there is tragedy outside our borders
Women are killed and gang raped
Because soldiers go by their own orders

Some are raped in front of family members
Just for the motive of humiliation
Millions are killed if they do not oblige
Experiencing dismemberment and castration

I wonder if the same solders would be distressed
If their mother or daughter was sodomized
While men took turns in a circle
As their precious love ones were victimized

Women are a gift from God
And are supposed to be taken as wives
Not to be used sexual toys
Discarded and taking their lives

# _My First Sex Teacher_

If you notice today in the news reports
Teachers spend less time in the classroom
And more in the courts

They seem to like them innocent and immature
Instead of teaching them values
They teach them how to be impure

How can a woman that's married
With three kids, and a perfect family?
Conspire to molest students
The same age as her own
Its immoral insanity

But since our society is saturated with sex
Being trapped in the closet
Guess who's next, who's coming to dinner?
A whore, a teacher, a molester, a sinner

# *One Man*

It's amazing how one man will dream
The other will wish
One will always hit his target
The other will miss
One plans well and organizes
The other downcast by circumstances and surprises

One man has faith, the other one doubt
One is constantly being ushered in
The other one kicked out
One man procrastinates
The other one is meticulous
One man is always prosperous
The other one ridiculous

One man will have a family
The other will remain single
One man will be content with one wife
The other is a playboy who has to mingle

# *When I Die*

When I die I don't need the recognition and applause
I need to hear well done for faithfulness for the cause
I don't need the plaques or any more awards
But I need to hear welcome home from the Lord of
Lords
I don't need anymore fancy designer clothes
Because I'm trading them all in for a blood dipped robe
I certainty need to know I will be able to enter
Where all flesh gets no glory and God is the center

I want to hear the angels singing, my family celebrating
While I overcame the world, they were patiently
waiting
If anyone ever says that life is always easy
I know they are just encouraging me, trying to please
me
Death should not be feared, instead embraced
Knowing you did your best when you ran this race
To welcome me home where there is no more sorrow
Or waking up facing the same problems tomorrow

# _Methods of Death_

Lethal gas from our lethal pass
Stoning, moaning, corpses groaning
Firing squads may seem odd
But the noose was never loose

Crucify, crucify the crowd would yell
Lethal injection would send inmates to Hell
The gallows were ready, the ax in hand steady
Sharp guillotines even crept upon the scenes

Old sparky was like a barbeque grill
An advanced method chosen for the kill
Drowning, dragging, beheadings, stabbings
Dismembered, eaten alive, how could you survive?

# _Counsel Me_

Why is it, those who know the least
Always say the most
They always want to counsel
And never fail to boast
But when you examine their life
They counsel from the books
Not from life's experience
Like being raised around robbers and crooks

They tell you about raising children
And never even conceived
Then it's onto marriage
And every word becomes harder to believe
We will receive your counsel
But first walk a day in our shoes
Then we will be receptive
When you spread the good news

# _Don't Shake My Hand_

I cannot begin to tell you how many times
I've been in a public stall
And what I've seen some men do
Will certainly make your skin crawl

I've seen some men in the restroom
Zip their pants and come off the commode
Walk to the door and open it
And my mind went into a disbelieving mode

They would open the door and walk out
As if to not even bother
And here I am staring at the sink
That is supplied with soap and water

How nasty can you be?
To ignore millions of germs
And have the audacity to shake someone's hands
Exposing them to viruses on your terms

*We then that are strong ought to bear the infirmities of the weak, and not to please ourselves.*

*Romans 15:1*

# *The Nag*

It's not surprising why some folks are lonely
They nag, and nag and nag and it's only
Always complaining, always temperamental
Sometimes lazy, sometimes differential
This is wrong, that is wrong
Different lyrics, same song

They bash their ex, complain about the sex
The bash every man, with no respect
They complain about what you wear
How you style your hair
How well you spend your cash
And yet they continue to bash

How you raise the children
How you mow the lawn
How the balance the checkbook
They go on and on and on

## _Learn The Distinction_

We will call the mediocre, great
Confuse love with hate
Call the zeros heroes
Confuse being cautious with being late

We think whores will make good wives
Money will change our lives
Serving any God would be beneficial
Oblivious it can be detrimental

We follow those not worth following
Embrace pride that's hard swallowing
A lie will sound more appealing
And confuse hard work
With wheeling and dealing

## *The Power of Two*

God gave you two feet to walk in your destiny
Two eyes to behold his glory
Two ears to hear and understand
Two hands to till and work the land
Two nostrils to breathe the fresh air
Two parents to show you they care
Two lips for an affectionate kiss
Two ankles for support and also two wrists
Two thumbs to assist when you hold
Two knees to bow for your soul
Two hands to create wealth
Two minds to be wise with our health
Two arms to caress and to embrace
But he did not give you the ability to be two faced

# *Shhhhhhh !*

When someone speaks negativity over your life
You can receive it and believe it
Or reject it and neglect it
I was a product of negative speaking
During childhood and adolescence
Those words spoken I began reaping
I was told repeatedly that I would always be a thug
So I sampled women, sampled liquor, and sampled
drugs
My subconscious mind received it and began to process
Year after year it was stress and more stress
I did not understand what in the world was taking place
Those negative words that were spoken
Could this be the case?

I chose to believe what was said like a fool
It was easy since my environment was a cesspool
I should have to them Shhhh! To please be quiet
Instead I listened and my flesh had a riot
I became rebellious, arrogant, would get angry and yell
And years later my outburst would send me to jail
If man didn't make you he cannot recreate you
God made you perfect so all man can do is mistake you

## *Anger Motivates*

Contrary to popular opinion not all anger is destructive
If used in the right manner it can be very conductive
Think of the mother who loses her son to a drunk driver
And births out the non-profit because of the rage inside
her
Or the father who becomes an activist due to abduction
This would not have happened if his life had no
interruptions

Have you heard the saying everything happens for a
reason
I will go one step further and say
It also happens in a particular season
Imagine you were at a bank and denied a loan
Let the anger work for you and start your own
We are only limited by our own fears
Life is short, and we have wasted far too many years

You will not cause things to happen until you are sick
and tired
Completely fed up and expired
Experience enough poverty and you will be motivated
to empower
Not only yourself but also others in the same hour
So don't always think all anger is destructive
If used in the right manner it can be very conductive

## *You Assume*

A notice to all credit agencies and collectors
The very one you put down just might be an investor
Never assume because someone was late on a bill
The are pitiful and deserve to be treated ill
You talk as if you know their whole life story
Based on a late payment, you place them in a category
That category is, those in society who always need
assistance
Unbeknownst to you we are actually the most persistent
You are content in your assistant manager position
Degrading those who possess the greatest vision

Be very careful whom you decide to degrade
Because you might actually be the one who needs aid
Remember the underdogs in society always rise
Always resilient, determined, and seeking the prize
The very ones who fell on hard times will also blow
your mind
So don't assume you know the outcome

## *Just Forgive*

Isn't it funny that God commands us to forgive
Yet we hold others hostage and not allow them to live
It may have been years since you were offended
You know you should forgive them
And it's always been intended
Instead you harbor ill feelings deep within your soul
You want God to bless you but your feelings are cold
Jesus said if you wouldn't forgive others
How can he forgive you?
God expect us to be like him, righteous and true

When you have been wronged it hurts beyond measure
It's hard to hold a grudge and at the same time have
pleasure
Forgiving is not always easy, but we can do it
With the strength of God at work we can get through it
Know that they are human, and people make mistakes
Jesus was on the cross and gave them a way of escape

Why are you still holding a grudge and wont budge?
Forgive and release it, walk in love and then cease it

He said Father forgive them they know not what they
do!

## *Hollywood Help Us*

Has marriage lost its luster and obligation to unity?
The answer is yes
Especially in the Hollywood community
The vows read for better or for worse
But as soon as you get ticked off
You are ready to disperse
Are you aware that the eyes of this world
Are always observing
We are like your customers, but what are you serving
Every time we see the news, we see another divorce
The world looks to you for a standard
But you are always off course

What has happened to upholding your commitments?

Hollywood please helps us
And shows some devotion
So we can silence the separations
And senseless commotion
We the people need an example
From the rich, well toned, glamorous and ample
Be faithful to your spouse for more than a week
Instead of affairs on the side, unnecessary and cheap

# *Jonah*

God told Jonah to go
But he was not quick to agree
Little did he know his greatest test
Would end up in the depths of the sea
When God told him to go
He gave precise directions
And because he went the opposite route
He was not under Gods protection
Although God was still watching over him
Jonah was reluctant to move as he was commanded
So the men on board threw him over
And he found himself stranded

He should have known better
Since God is relentless
He held out as long as he could
Until he was confused and senseless
The whale swallowed him up
And spit him out on the shore
Yet he was angry and still displeased
And his cry God didn't ignore
God said to Jonah why you are upset
He let the sun beat down upon him
Until he was covered in sweat
In the final chapter Jonah uttered a few more words
God answered him back and that was all you heard

*Ye have not chosen me, but I have chosen you, and ordained you, that ye should go and bring forth fruit, and that your fruit should remain; that whatsoever ye shall ask of the Father in my name, he may give it to you.*

*John 15:16*

# *The Benefits of Marriage*

I come to find out that with marriage comes prosperity
Two like minds walking in agreement brings clarity
Same understanding and never off track
You always have a friend to watch your back

When you are committed there is no threat of disease
Sex is wholesome and pure; your mind is at ease
Proverbs 31 says she does her husband good and not
harm
All thee days of her life she keeps him warm
When you are blessed with a spouse
Who is honest and ambitious
You can give them your trust without being suspicious
When two walk together
There is double income and double resources
Double the anointing to counterattack the divorces

But during this union there must be some loyalty
Like learning to treat one another just like royalty
The secrets of a husband and wife
Should stay just that, secret
Meaning what was told to you
Is private and you should keep it

# *I'm Opposed*

When something bad happens to you
Stop saying why me
Opposition opens blind eyes so you can see
Without some obstacle to continuously oppose
We become paralyzed with fear like something froze
Accept the opposition, and continue to thrive
Know that you represent God and come alive

When you are denied
Let it cause you to press in even the more
The more no's you hear will cause you to soar
When the spirit of God resides in you
You cannot be stopped
Despite the negative words of others
You are the cream of the crop

Never let race, circumstances or gender
Ever, ever, ever, cause you to surrender

# The Forgotten 50's

Joseph Stalin is finally laid to rest
From Here to Eternity is an Oscars best
Deborah Kerr and Burt Lancaster
Over 2000 dead of a flooding disaster
Lucille Ball is an international success
Albert Einstein and James Dean both laid to rest

Rosa Parks fed up with sitting in the back
Refusing to give up her seat to liberate blacks
Teenage rebellion, the story of Rebel without a Cause
As Christian Dior and Bogeys death made us pause
Elvis would make the girls scream and holler
Minimum wage was raised from 75 cents to a dollar

Castro leads a Cuban Revolution
As the new Barbie doll gets a US distribution
We said farewell to Billie Holiday and Errol Flynn
America was a great nation but still engulfed in sin
Alaska joined the USA by becoming the 49th state
Was Dwight D. Eisenhower a good president caused a
debate?

# *I'll Have My Mansion Now*

Jesus said he would go away
And prepare me a heavenly home
A place of my eternal rest
That I could call my own
He said it would be a mansion
And not a rundown shack
Built by the carpenter himself
And the foundation has no cracks
Marble floors, pavements made of gold
Not listed among the realtors
Because the property is sold
I'll have my mansion now!

The yard is well manicured
The edges nicely trimmed
As I walk around in a flawless
White robe nicely hemmed
This feels good knowing
I sent ahead the materials needed
I spoke while on earth, paid in full
So the property is already deeded
My property value steadily rises
Because my neighbor takes care of his home
We are all together one big family
And never ever alone
I'll have my mansion now!

## _Poor Samson_

He was given the strength of Clark Kent
Fully aware he was appointed and sent
And just like Clark a lady stole his heart
Yet she played on his affections and it tore it apart
And yet Sampson was partly to blame
Playing with fire is such a deadly game
Because he told Delilah the forbidden
The secret of his God given strength
That was to remain hidden
But once he gave his precious pearls to the swine
The spirit of God departed and he literally lost his mind

# *The HELL Deception*

All throughout history men have taught
That hell is not a real habitation
Demons will purposely confuse
People with the wrong information
When the truth comes forth
They cause those to become hypnotic
Turning sane men into the psychotic
They preach the horrors of Hell are a happy haven
Knowing the flesh will be picked by the ravens

It's been said that Hell exists in your mind
It's not a real place that you can locate and find
It's very real and constantly enlarging
For all those who have sought out evil, it will be
rewarding

It only makes sense, why teach that it does not exist
So you will miss heaven and abide in the abyss
Philosophers throughout the years
Being wise in their eyes
They have their own logic and reasoning
But these are all lies

# *Are You Really Free*

Even when liberty was declared amid the blacks
During slavery
Fear was paralyzing to the mind
And took dominion over bravery
Some chose to stay behind
In the master's domain
Like the children of Israel
Leaving Egypt's bondage chains
Many believe they are free
Based on the Emancipation Proclamation
Unaware the state of the mind
To different variations

They said to the slave, "You are now free"
But the slave looked upon the vast land
And said I disagree
Just like God told Joshua
To be of good courage and posses the land
A slave mindset refuses to take risk
And does not understand
Why should we be free?
When it's safe in the comfort zone
Remaining average, content, hostile, and all alone

# Is My Opinion Too Strong

There is nothing I love more than a great discussion
To engage the intellect without any interruption
Some can debate well, while some will be offended
But if they give their input, the conversation is perfectly
blended

I understand that some people will feel intimidated
If the bulk of the conversation is being dominated
All intellect is brainpower and intelligence
Some have more knowledge
Which makes their words more relevant

This world would be bland
If we all had the same observation
Stifling our God given brilliancy
With the same information

## _I Love the Underdogs_

I love stories of ordinary people
Those who became great financially
Coming from the depths of poverty
To a net worth substantially
These are the ones society
Disregards, and condones
They undermine your vision and also disowns

Years later you always read
Articles of the underdogs rising
A successful corporation
A seven-figure income
And yet it's never surprising
God said whatever you find your hand to do
Do it with all your might
He said write the vision down
Make it plain, and never let it out of sight

*Draw nigh to God, and he will draw nigh to you, Cleanse your hands, ye sinners; and purify your hearts, ye double minded*

*James 4:8*

## _The Remedies For Your Sickness_

Ripe avocadoes, ruby red tomatoes
Steaming fresh broccoli
And piping hot jalapenos

Black beans, red beans
Brown rice, sounds nice
Celery, onions, vine grown blackberries
A clove of garlic a day, frozen blueberries

Baked, steamed, or grilled fish
Preferably salmon or tilapia
Which is a favorite dish

Mushrooms, carrots, bell peppers, and beets
And when you have a sweet tooth
Use pure honey as a treat

Break out the dark chocolate
When its time to snack
Or an oatmeal granola bar
To help keep you on track

## *Lead Us Not Into Temptation*

To all the women we love
Known as our spouses
Lead us not into temptation
In our very own houses
I'm not in the mood
I'm too tired, not tonight
The excuses are getting old
Out of mind and out of sight
Just like you need love
Commitment and affection
We need action
In the occurrence of an erection

We are men, very sexual creatures
We are your students, you are our teachers

We chose you to marry you
To carry our mighty name
And we would love for your sexuality
To be passionate and the same

## _Their Definition of Black_

To be black means to be dark
Not only in skin but permanently marked
Burnt, scarred, barbequed, charred
Hopeless, helpless, and heartless
Aggressive by nature, loud and rude
Illiterate with words and plus bad attitudes
Most violent offenders and the great pretenders
Pretending to be educated, but self-elevated
Every time other races see their faces
They are quick to move from their spaces
Major sports and rap figures
But still just niggers, defeated, and cheated
No wisdom, no vision, no goals, no decisions
They claim blessings, yet still has poverty
Never miss a day of church and still play the lottery
But yet they say God is good

They love to drink wine, sit back and recline
Gossip on the phone way past nine
Because after all I'm glad she got what she deserved
Said the gossiper!

Bad credit scores, the women dress like whores
Less money spent on their future than in department
stores

Descendants of big momma's and big daddies
With fat stomachs and big caddies

But what did big momma and big daddy ever achieve
Other than cholesterol, which is not hard to believe
After all they say were lazy and crazy

Fornicators, perpetrators, but never creators
Unsettled in the mind, and always attempting to bind
The enemy, for what reason, they say it's their season
But their fruit never seems to ripen

A mouth full of gold, as they continuously sell their
soul
They claim to have destiny, but our children of Satan
So if they're waiting to exhale, let them keep on
waiting
You've heard of black outs, black plagues, even black
mail
Black is negative in meaning, so it's no wonder they
fail

## *1 is The Loneliest Number*

God created man to have friends
To set trends and to make ends
He created man to uphold, to be bold

One will chase a thousand
Two will but ten thousand to flight
You can accomplish much alone
But with two you increase your might

One will have wisdom, while two can be wiser
1 can be a great thinker
The other a great advisor

## *Whose Sin is Greater*

Is there one sin greater than another?
Such as loving yourself and hating your brother
Would my lying be equivalent to your cheating?
How about my lust versus your overeating?

Another's profanity in contrast to your
promiscuousness
To say one sin is greater is ridiculous

If I steal, and yet you are a liar
Without repentance
We both face the threat of Hell fire

We are not judges adorned in robes
With gavels in hand, anointed to probe

# *Plantation Behavior*

Two hundred years ago
They master's put the dark blacks against the light
The weak ones against the might
The young men against the old
The ones who kept secrets against those who told
The put women against the men
The outside ones against those who were in
The good looking against the unattractive
The peaceful against the combative

In the fields all day, hungry and on display
Whipped for a lack of production
Much profanity and corruption
Even though it has been decades
Since we were in captivity
Could this have affected relations between blacks?
And our sensitivities

There is a fight to see who will get the last word
Instead of having one in authority
Someone just has to be heard

Women are now the head
Because men are completely degraded
Exited out of the family and also separated

# *You Remind Me*

Some people will do things for you
And will remind you on a daily basis
If it weren't for me, you wouldn't have this
They reiterate every time you see their faces
I paid this bill, and I paid that one too
And if it weren't for me, what would you do

My mom use to always tell me
If you did it for me, don't keep bragging
Because that would put you in a category
Of a nuisance who keeps on nagging

If you lent me the money
Then accept it as a good deed
You don't have to tell the whole world
You helped me out, when I was in need

## _Based On a True Story_

One summer night as I drove through Alabama
I pulled in Chevron to get some fuel
A racist officer approached me
Who at first seemed to be cool

He ask me this question
"Boy," Why are you driving through Alabama?
I replied in a rather calm voice
I'm on my way to Atlanta

He said, why couldn't you find another route to take?
I said sir this is the only route I know
So why don't you give me a break

The whole time he was talking he kept his hand on his
gun
Hoping I would smart off to him
Or be completely foolish and run
It taught me a lesson that night
That some folks are still stuck in their habits
Playing mental plantation games
Still chasing blacks like rabbits

## _Spreading_

We tell our children to sow their wild oats and be
cantankerous
Have as many sex partners and be adventurous
We use phrases like boys will be boys
Mischievous at best, playing with their toys
Unfortunately those toys just happen to be girls
Spreading their seed around the world

But I saw in the Bible where eight year olds became
kings
Walking in wisdom, amongst other things
They ruled kingdoms, not yet in their teens
Now ask yourself what all this means

What I'm saying is children can be established early
Having a relationship with God
And understanding he alone is worthy

Following the ungodly only leads to destruction
And their impressionable mind needs no corruption

*For God shall bring every work into judgment, with every secret thing, whether it be good, or whether it be evil.*

*Ecclesiastes 12:14*

# _Dictation_

If you don't take out time to plan your goals
Society will dictate your compensation and roles
You will have to settle for what has been given
Society will also determine your standard of living

If you are irresponsible
Write down every goal and make it clear and plane
Charter your path down every lane

When you see those around you
Who are continuously poor
Society dictated to them
The inability to soar

If you don't make your rules
You will live by those created
Following the repetition
And never liberated

## _Don't Get Bitter, Get Better_

Just incase you didn't get the promotion
Or the applause
Lift your head and fight for the cause
If your vision has been delayed
Don't get bitter just get better
Free your mind and get it together

Life is too short incase you hadn't noticed
To dwell on irrelevant things
To deter your focus
Don't get bitter, just get better
Free your mind and get it together

## *The Profession*

She claims she has to feed her kids
So she strips
Once the dollar bill is waived
She thrust her thighs and hips

Up and down the pole she goes
While drunk men call her kind project Hoe's
Southern Hip Hop plays in the rear of the club
Then she drops it like it's hot
High off elicit drugs

Surely this woman has lost her individuality
Choosing this profession
Even though she is making money
She is clueless to her own oppression

# _Strike_

He strikes her with his fist
Then he says I love you
I will never do it again

She believes him this time
Although he confessed it before
Convincing herself this is her friend

He comes home drunk
As violent as a lion
Who's trapped in a den
Strikes her a second time
And says I'll never do it again

He strikes in the face
Strikes her in the head
Strikes her one to many times
Until he strikes her dead

# *Time Stands Still*

Time Stands Still
When you are breathing, receiving and believing
But it moves fast when you are lying, stealing
And deceiving
Time Stands Still
When you are thinking, investing and planning
But it moves fast when you are abusive, controlling
And demanding
Time Stands Still
When you are wise, ambitious and wealthy
But it moves fast when you are greedy, proud
And unhealthy
Time Stands Still
When you worship and spend time in prayer
But it moves fast when you are selfish and don't have a
care
Time Stands Still
When you seek and find that one true friend
But it moves fast when you gossip, and in their face
grin
Time Stands still
When you are meditating, and concentrating
But it moves fast when you are livid with rage and
contemplating
Time Stands Still
When you laugh, wonder, and smile

But it moves fast when your behavior is unpredictable
and vile
Time Stands Still
When you are clean, honest and sober
But it moves oh so fast then its over!

# *Politically Incorrect*

Politically Incorrect, absolutely, always
Forward to future tense
Rewind to ancient days
Following the crowd, never
Filled with Gods wisdom, too clever

They say be quiet, raise your voice higher
When they try to extinguish your flame
Start a fire

Although shipwrecked and beaten
Faith will never weaken
Stand up and never sit down
Airborne and never Hell bound

Look you enemy straight in the eye
A dead man can't be afraid to die

## *What Are You Waiting For*

There was a man who lay by the pool for 38 years
Afraid to move forward due to numerous fears
He relied on others to meet his need
But man overlooked him
And would never perform any deeds

But Jesus asked him, after seeing his condition
Wilt thou be made whole
Since he was willing
Immediately he stood up, bold

In other words, there's never a reason
To sit idle and wait on man
God has given us power
To overcome and stand
Any test, any trial, any tribulation
He is our ever-present help
The God of our salvation

# _It's The Simple Things_

Did you know that wisdom is hidden in creation?
And wealth is even buried within this nation
Thousands of medicinal cures are hidden within plants
And you can become wealthy by observing ants

It's the simple things that we fail to notice
Because bigger issues deter our focus
Did you know that a positive attitude
Can be a cure for cancer
Your subconscious mind will release every answer

Did you know that the favor of God
Is worth more than cash
Anonymous men become wealthy
From another mans trash

Did you know vitality is in the forest?
Diamonds are in the soil
An antibiotic can come from bread
If you allow it to spoil

Miracles are all around us, if you just pay attention!

# *Boyfriends Versus Husbands*

A boyfriend may stay out late
A husband will remain at home
Husbands usually cuddle after sex
Boyfriends continue to roam

Husbands are great providers
A boyfriend may want it 50, 50
Husbands tend to spend on their families
Boyfriends tend to be thrifty

Husbands choose to marry
To enjoy his wife's pleasure
Boyfriends chose to forego ceremonies
But still like tapping into treasures

Husbands like long drives
Boyfriends like drive-thru's
Husbands know the important facts
Boyfriends are missing vital clues

# Notes

# Notes

# Notes

# Notes

# Recommended Reading

## Thought Provoking Poems and Poetry for Positive and Powerful People vol.1
By Sylvester R. Cade
$10.95
ISBN 9781432706180

## Taking Care of Business
By Lee Jenkins
$13.99
ISBN 13 978-0-8024-4016-7
ISBN 0-8024-4016-9

## An Enemy Called Average
By John L. Mason
ISBN 1-56292-046-4

## The Man God Uses
By Henry and Tom Blackaby
$15.99
ISBN 080542145-9
ISBN 9780805421453

## Making Your Dreams Come True
By Marcia Wieder
ISBN 0-609-60608-5
ISBN 9780609606087

If you are in need of prayer

Send all requests to:

**Church On The Rock Matt 16:18**
**Christian Center**
**9041 Cullen Blvd**
**Houston, TX 77051**

**713.733.0703 office**
**churchontherockmatt.16.18@juno.org**

**Bernard &Vanessa Womack Pastors**

## To Contact Us

*By mail*

**Kingdom World Enterprises™**
**3418 Chateau Crest Ct**
**Houston, TX 77047**

*By fax*
**832.553.2747**

*By Email*
**tcade@houston.rr.com**

**Sylvester R. Cade**
**President / CEO**

# Kingdom

**Publishing**

**Marketing/ Advertising/ Motivational Speaking**

*Uncommon, Uncut*

www.ingramcontent.com/pod-product-compliance
Lightning Source LLC
LaVergne TN
LVHW011353080426
835511LV00005B/264